SHARK

FACE-OFF!

Scholastic Inc.

Contents

Great hammerhead shark

Dive in!

Sharks are the most feared—and misunderstood—creatures on the planet. They are certainly wild—no one ever tamed a shark! But they are so much more than just killing machines. They are the ultimate survivors. Their ancestors were swimming the world's oceans 450 million years ago, long before the dinosaurs appeared, even longer before the first mammal! Yet they are still here today puzzling us and frightening us, still the ocean's peak predators.

BATTLE SCORE

These sharks are perfectly camouflaged for attack and defense on the reef.

ATTACK SCORE:	**5/10**
DEFENSE SCORE:	**7/10**
LENGTH:	**3.5 ft**
POWER MOVE:	**Ambush hunter**

Check out the battle scores for each ocean creature and discover their unique strengths. Who do you think would win if they faced off? Who has the best stats and the best power moves? Which ones are your favorites? Do you agree with the scores? You can ask friends or family members what they think, too!

All kinds of creatures
The 250,000 or so known ocean creatures include some of the most spectacular on Earth.

Leopard seals (p 46) are the only seals to regularly prey on warm-blooded animals, like smaller seals!

The superfast sailfish (p 58) keeps its sail folded, but raises it during an attack.

Sharks and much more

There are more than 500 shark species. In this book, you'll meet not only the most famous, such as the awesomely powerful great white, but others you might not know, such as the kitefin shark, which glows in the dark! You'll also meet a host of other predators that share the ocean with sharks, from fierce mammals to other fast fish to tiny animals that can punch a hole through your shoe. Dive in!

Wobbegong sharks are ambush predators. Camouflaged on the seabed, they lunge when prey comes by!

The mantis shrimp (p 39) can spring its fist out and punch prey with the force of a speeding bullet.

Beware! The Portuguese man o' war (p 60) can sting you even with a severed tendril!

Peak predators

Never underestimate a shark! Some are harmless. Some are tiny. But big sharks like the tiger shark are ultimate predators, every inch honed for hunting—supersenses for tracking prey; strong, sleek bodies to chase it down; and deadly jaws for the final kill.

Dorsal fin keeps the shark stable.

Upper jaw is only loosely attached to the skull, so jaws can be shot forward as the mouth opens.

The nose is used for smelling, not breathing.

Water flows smoothly over toothlike scales, called "dermal denticles," that cover sharks' bodies.

Most sharks have five gill slits; some have six or even seven.

Shark attacked

For 450 million years, sharks have survived everything nature had to throw at them. But now humans are putting them in danger by catching them in our nets and damaging their homes. In 2021, a study of 31 shark and ray species showed 24 are threatened with extinction, and 3 famous species—the oceanic whitetip shark, and the scalloped and great hammerhead sharks—are close to being lost altogether.

Pectoral fins are for lift and stability. Sharks can only swim forward, as these fins can't bend upward!

Sharks have at least 6 senses. Besides smell, touch, taste, sight, and hearing, they can detect pressure and electricity.

Large, oily livers help sharks stay afloat.

The skeleton is made from cartilage, the same sort of material that's in your nose. It's light and flexible, so sharks need less energy to move.

The tail, or caudal fin, is moved from side to side to power the shark forward.

Vision: Sharks have similar eyes to mammals, but they also have a reflective layer of cells that help them to see in dim and murky water. Sharks can detect contrasts of light and shadow, and some species see in color.

Smell: Sharks are famous for their amazing sense of smell. Some species can detect a single drop of blood in the water from a quarter of a mile away!

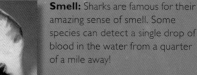

Touch: Shark skin is very sensitive. Sharks have a "lateral line" of pores down their sides that can detect the direction and movement of prey as far as 820 feet away.

Taste: Sharks may take a "test bite" out of prey. Their taste buds determine if it's suitable to eat. If not, it's spat out and the prey is left alone.

Hearing: Small openings on sharks' heads lead to inner ears, which can hear sounds from miles away. They can pick up lower-frequency sounds made by injured or dying creatures.

Electroreception: Tiny gel-filled pores on a shark's head, called "ampullae of Lorenzini," can detect the electrical signals that animals create when their muscles contract. They can even pick up a heartbeat.

Rows of teeth

Sharks have an unlimited supply of teeth, set in rows, with no jawbone. Every time a shark loses a tooth, the one behind replaces it. Sharks can go through thousands of teeth in a lifetime! Not all shark teeth are pointed like daggers. Flattened teeth are needed to crush shells. Needlelike teeth grip struggling prey.

Sand tiger

Tiger

The Port Jackson shark has front teeth with cusps for gripping prey and flat, back teeth for crushing shells.

Ocean arenas

The oceans might look like just a mass of blue water. But for sea animals, it's an unbelievably rich and varied place to live. We know of nearly 250,000 different sea creatures, and there may be two million or more! Each one has its own special place and lifestyle, from the tiniest bacteria to the largest animal on the planet: the blue whale.

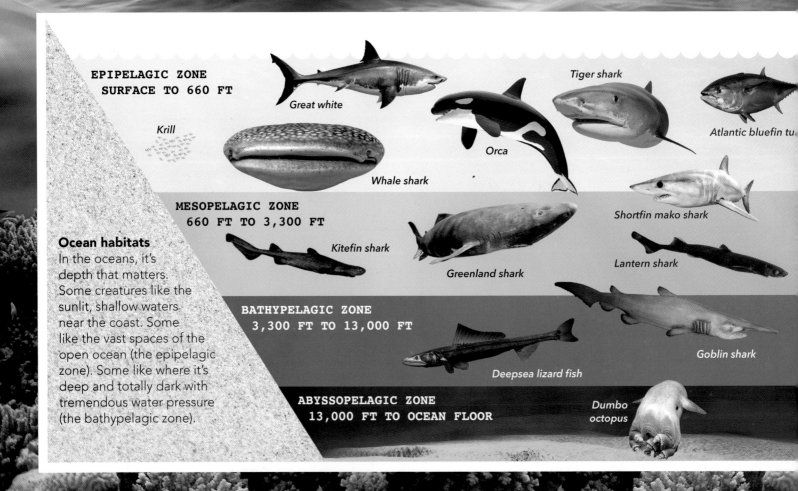

EPIPELAGIC ZONE
SURFACE TO 660 FT

Krill

Great white

Whale shark

Orca

Tiger shark

Atlantic bluefin tu...

MESOPELAGIC ZONE
660 FT TO 3,300 FT

Kitefin shark

Greenland shark

Shortfin mako shark

Lantern shark

BATHYPELAGIC ZONE
3,300 FT TO 13,000 FT

Deepsea lizard fish

Goblin shark

ABYSSOPELAGIC ZONE
13,000 FT TO OCEAN FLOOR

Dumbo octopus

Ocean habitats
In the oceans, it's depth that matters. Some creatures like the sunlit, shallow waters near the coast. Some like the vast spaces of the open ocean (the epipelagic zone). Some like where it's deep and totally dark with tremendous water pressure (the bathypelagic zone).

Jungles of the sea

Thousands of species make their homes, or hide out, in coral reefs growing offshore in sunlit, tropical waters. The Great Barrier Reef, off the northeast coast of Australia, is longer than the West Coast of the US! The reefs are built up over long periods from the mineral skeletons of colonies of animals called "polyps," that look a little like sea anemones. Sadly, reefs are being damaged beyond repair by rising temperatures worldwide, as well as pollution.

Big lemon sharks hunt in packs on sandy seabeds, and a feeding frenzy follows!

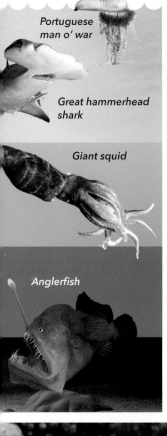

Portuguese man o' war

Great hammerhead shark

Giant squid

Anglerfish

GREAT WHITE VS

Great white sharks are the ultimate ocean hunters. They're large and fast with a top speed of 25 miles per hour (mph). Their sharp teeth slice through flesh, ripping it off in chunks when the shark shakes its head. But great whites aren't the mindless killers that they're often made out to be. Rare attacks on swimmers may be driven by curiosity, not rage.

BATTLE SCORE
Highly intelligent, with a torpedo-shaped body and strong tail for acceleration.

ATTACK SCORE: **10/10**
DEFENSE SCORE: **9/10**
LENGTH: **20 ft**
POWER MOVE: **Fierce bite**

Great whites have an upper jaw of 23 to 28 bladelike teeth and a lower jaw of 21 to 25.

Ambush from below
A great white hunts mainly in the early morning or evening, when light bounces off the water. It sneaks up underneath its prey, then makes a sudden lunge, even breaching 10 feet right out of the water.

- **NAME:** *Carcharodon carcharias* (jagged teeth point)
- **HABITAT:** Open water, mainly warm coastal
- **DIET:** Fish, seals, seabirds, turtles
- **LOCATION:** Worldwide

Liver please!
When orcas kill sharks, they don't eat the whole animal. They're very picky! They bite a small hole in the shark's side and eat up the liver, which is super rich in healthy oils.

ORCA

These dolphins are big, strong, and fast, but their biggest asset is how they hunt in teams. There may be dozens of them hunting a young blue whale or beating their flukes together to create a wave and wash a seal off the ice into the water. Clever and social in many ways, research with drones shows that, like us, orcas often make special friends with another orca of the same age.

The male orca's dorsal fin is as tall as an adult human.

- **NAME:** *Orcinus orca*
  (god of the netherworld, barrel-shaped)
- **HABITAT:** Coastal waters, mainly cool
- **DIET:** Fish, seabirds, marine mammals
- **LOCATION:** Worldwide

Dinner is sealed
Orcas are top of their food chain and feed on fish, seabirds, and sea lions. They can breach right out of the water and snap up seals resting on ice. Orcas live and hunt in groups, or pods, with up to 55 members. Pods mainly stay together, and don't like mixing with other pods. Orcas are mammals, like all whales and dolphins, so they surface at intervals to breathe air.

Flipping sharks!
Orcas eat sharks, chasing them at speeds of more than 34 mph. Some individuals are known to kill great whites. How they do this is not known for sure, but it seems that they somehow manage to turn the sharks onto their backs, making them immobile, so they drown.

TIGER SHARK

Tiger sharks are second only to great whites in the shark ranks. They're incredible hunters and scavengers. They're also fearless. Recent research shows that while most sharks flee from shallows when a hurricane approaches, tigers actually seem to relish the rough and tumble—and the mess of dead animals that wash up!

Stripy skin
Tiger sharks get their name from dark, tigerlike stripes down their bodies.

Tiger sharks hunt at night alone, able to sense the electrical signals given off by prey in the dark.

Danger!
Tiger sharks are second only to great whites for attacks on swimmers, and are much feared by surfers in places such as Hawaii.

The teeth are shaped perfectly for cutting and sawing (see p 7).

NAME: *Galeocerdo cuvier* (Cuvier's fox shark)
HABITAT: Warm coastal waters
DIET: Mainly fish, very diverse
LOCATION: Temperate, tropical oceans

Nothing left
There's no messing with a tiger shark. It might circle its prey and nudge it before an attack. But once it strikes, everything is eaten—bones, guts, the works. That's why it often ends up with a stomach full of trash!

VS LEMON SHARK

A yellow-ish shade on top, lemon sharks are hard to spot swimming over sandy seabeds. In mangrove swamps and coral reefs, their yellow-ish camouflage makes them effective, sneaky hunters. They may be among the smartest sharks, forming bonds and sharing information.

Shark party
Lemon sharks are quite social and hang out together in special areas where they can meet a mate. They give birth to live babies, who spend their first 7 to 8 years safely in a "nursery" in a lagoon or a bay, learning how to hunt.

Lemon sharks may hunt in a group and take part in feeding frenzies.

- **NAME:** *Negaprion brevirostris* (blunt back teeth, short beak)
- **HABITAT:** Warm, shallow waters
- **DIET:** Fish, seabirds
- **LOCATION:** Atlantic, Eastern Pacific

Lemon sharks have never been known to kill humans.

Lemons squeezed
Because they live for so long in the shallows, lemon sharks are often targeted for fishing, and their habitats are damaged by human coastal development. Sadly, in some areas, they are in danger of extinction.

HAMMERHEAD VS

The great hammerhead is the top predator among other sharks and rays in coastal waters, and vital in keeping their numbers in check. Its superwide head is actually a scanner! It's filled with sensors (ampullae of Lorenzini), which pick up electrical signals from stingrays hiding in the sand.

Hammerheads aren't aggressive toward humans; there have been few attacks.

The hammer, or cephalofoil, is very flat with a central notch.

- **NAME:** *Sphyrna mokarran* (hammer big)
- **HABITAT:** Tropical, warm temperate coastal
- **DIET:** Fish
- **LOCATION:** Worldwide

Wide eyes
Because their eyes are so far apart, hammerheads have phenomenal binocular (3-D) vision, up to three times better than pointy-nosed sharks. The wide head isn't just a scanner; it's a weapon. The shark uses it to pin rays against the seafloor as it bites.

Journey time
Hammerheads are some of the world's greatest migrators. They spend the summer months in cooler waters, but swim 1,800 miles or more to reach warmer waters for the winter. Hammerheads have become very rare, as they have been fished for their fins.

COMMON THRESHER

BATTLE SCORE
The thresher's most useful weapon is its tail, but it's also very speedy.

ATTACK SCORE: **6/10**
DEFENSE SCORE: **7/10**
LENGTH: **Up to 19 ft**
POWER MOVE: **Agility**

There's no mistaking this shark. About half the length of its body is the caudal fin, or tail. The tail is used to herd fish into little groups. The thresher can then whip its tail over its head at 30 mph and bring it down to deliver a stunning blow. Very few predators will tackle this big, fast fish, though an orca might. It's in the mackerel shark family, alongside the great white and the makos.

The top side of the tail is longer than the bottom side.

The shark has 32 to 53 upper, and 25 to 50 lower rows of small, curved, sharp teeth.

Giant leap
One of the great athletes among sharks, the common thresher will leap, or breach, right out of the water. It may make quick turns in the air, like dolphins do. It's not entirely known why these fish breach, but it might be to shock and confuse their prey, and it's helpful in removing parasites.

An internal heat exchange system keeps the shark warmer than the surrounding water.

NAME: *Alopias vulpinus* (foxy fox)
HABITAT: Coastal, open water
DIET: Schooling fish, squid
LOCATION: Temperate, tropical oceans

Shark babies
Many sharks lay eggs, like the Port Jackson shark (p 37). Some, like the lemon shark (p 13), give birth to live young nourished by a placenta while they develop. Others, like the thresher shark, give birth to live young that are nourished first by a yolk sac and then by undeveloped eggs.

BASKING SHARK

This is the world's second-largest fish, with a mouth that's 3 feet or more wide and a pointed snout. But its teeth are tiny, and its mouth gapes wide only to take in 2,000 tons of water an hour, containing the microscopic plankton on which it feeds. Despite its size, it's a gentle, harmless creature.

Basking sharks can jump right out of the water and roll 360 degrees!

Sun lovers
Basking sharks are named for how they drift slowly along near the sunlit surface where they feed. They migrate thousands of miles in search of the best plankton. But no one is entirely sure where they go in winter.

The shark filters out plankton with gill rakers covered in mucus.

- **NAME:** *Cetorhinus maximus* (greatest monsternose)
- **HABITAT:** Cool waters
- **DIET:** Plankton
- **LOCATION:** All temperate oceans

Basking sharks may be scarred from encounters with lampreys or cookiecutter sharks.

Finished off
Basking sharks are so big and slow, they are easy to catch. Sadly, they are sometimes caught only to have their fins removed and then thrown back into the water to drown. Perhaps 100 million sharks of all species are killed by finning each year.

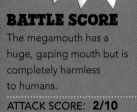
VS MEGAMOUTH

The megamouth shark is named for its round, monster mouth, sometimes over 4 feet wide! But like the basking shark, its mouth is used only for filtering tiny plankton out of the water. This is a very mysterious shark. Despite its size, it was only first recorded in 1976, and there have been barely a hundred sightings since.

NAME: *Megachasma pelagios*
(great cave of the sea)
HABITAT: Deep and shallow waters
DIET: Plankton, small fish, jellyfish
LOCATION: Temperate, tropical oceans

The huge mouth has rubbery-looking lips and 50 or more rows of teeth in each jaw.

Deep life
The megamouth comes up during the day to catch plankton near the surface, but it spends most of the time down in the deep ocean, which is why it is so hard to spot.

Spot a megamouth
Megamouths are seen so rarely that scientists have a record of all 99 official sightings up until 2018. Most have been caught accidentally in fishing nets or washed up on the beach. Their only known natural predator is the sperm whale.

Sperm whale

WHALE SHARK VS

Whale sharks are fish, not whales, and they're the biggest fish in the world—30 feet or more long! The only animals that grow bigger are giant squid and actual whales. Whale sharks aren't predators, though, just filter-feeders with tiny teeth.

Open wide
Whale sharks feed in three ways: swimming slowly, mouth open, straining plankton from the water; floating vertically and sucking in prey-rich water; actively sucking while swimming, in a method known as "ram-filter" feeding.

The skin on the back of a whale shark is six inches thick!

Each whale shark has a unique checkerboard pattern of spots and stripes on its back.

- **NAME:** *Rhincodon typus* (raspy tooth type)
- **HABITAT:** Warm temperate, tropical surface waters
- **DIET:** Plankton, small fish, fish eggs
- **LOCATION:** Worldwide except Mediterranean

Sir Fish!
The whale shark has different names around the world. In Madagascar, it's called "marokintana" or "many stars" for the spots on its back. In Vietnam, it's called "Ca Ong" or "Sir Fish." In Japan, it's known as "jinbei-zame," *jinbei* being a type of traditional summer clothing.

NURSE SHARK

Nurse sharks are the most laid back of all sharks. While most sharks need to keep moving to breathe, nurse sharks like a quiet life. By day, they just lie around on the seabed. By night, they amble through shallow waters, slurping up food from the sand and between rocks using their incredible powers of suction.

Two barbels, with taste buds, are dragged over the seafloor to detect prey. The little teeth take a toll from crushing shellfish; new ones continuously replace worn-out old ones.

Daytime rest
During the day, up to 40 nurse sharks can be seen resting together, sometimes piled on top of one another! They have special muscles that draw water into their mouths and over their gills so they can breathe while staying still.

Sometimes, the shark moves its pectoral fins to walk along the sand!

- **NAME:** *Ginglymostoma cirratum* (hinged mouth and ringlets)
- **HABITAT:** Intertidal, reefs, mangroves
- **DIET:** Fish, crustaceans, mollusks
- **LOCATION:** Eastern Pacific, E. and W. Atlantic

Baby name
Nobody knows how nurse sharks got their name. Some people think it's because their slurping and sucking sounds a little like a nursing baby.

ZEBRA SHARK VS

Zebra sharks are named for the stripes they have as youngsters—their scientific name is *tigrinum*, meaning "tigers." As they grow older, their stripes turn into leopard spots. Confused? That's the idea! The stripes and spots are camouflage from predators, like larger sharks.

BATTLE SCORE
Their sandy color and stripes and spots make them hard to see.

ATTACK SCORE: **4/10**
DEFENSE SCORE: **5/10**
LENGTH: **8 ft**
POWER MOVE:
Clever camouflage

A flexible body and narrow head means this shark can wriggle into tight crevices.

Seafloor vacuum
This suction feeder creeps over the seabed, vacuuming up prey hidden in the sand and in crevices in the reef. Zebra sharks hunt at night. Most of the day, they lie on the seafloor, facing into the current, making it easier to pump water over their gills to breathe.

- **NAME:** *Stegostoma tigrinum* (hidden mouth of the tiger)
- **HABITAT:** Warm coastal shallows
- **DIET:** Shellfish, shrimp, small fish
- **LOCATION:** Indian, Western Pacific

Zebras, leopards, and tigers
Because their pattern changes, zebra sharks are sometimes called "zebra" or "tiger" sharks when they are young, and "leopard" sharks when older. But beware—there is also a shark called the "leopard shark" (a kind of houndshark), and also a "tiger shark"! So look at the Latin name!

Leopard shark

ORNATE WOBBEGONG

A small shark with a big name! It's "ornate" because it looks like a very fancy, frilly piece of old carpet. *Wobbegong* is an Indigenous Australian word for "shaggy beard"—it has a beard-like fringe. All this camouflage is perfect for a sit-and-wait ambush predator on the reef.

Ambush predator
During the day, the wobbegong lies still, its shaggy shape making it almost invisible among the seaweed and coral. At night, it stays motionless, waiting for prey to pass close by, then grabs it with a quick snap of its jaws.

The wobbegong will give waders and fishers a bite if they disturb it in a tidepool.

Tassels aid camouflage and act as sensors.

NAME: *Orectolobus ornatus* (long lobed and ornate)
HABITAT: Warm coastal waters
DIET: Fish, crustaceans, octopus
LOCATION: East coast of Australia

Carpet sharks
Ornate wobbegongs aren't the only wobbegongs. In fact, there are 12 different kinds. The ornate is one of the shaggiest, and they are all shaggy, bottom-dwelling "carpet sharks"—that is, sharks that are patterned like old carpets. Whale sharks, zebra sharks, and nurse sharks are also carpet sharks.

Ornate wobbegong

VS

BATTLE SCORE

Angel sharks are well camouflaged and have explosive bursts of speed.

ATTACK SCORE: 6/10

DEFENSE SCORE: 5/10

LENGTH: 8 ft

POWER MOVE:
Burst of speed

With wide, triangular fins and a very, very flat shape, the common angel shark looks just like a ray. Its shape is perfect for lying still and unseen on the seafloor, especially if it buries itself a little in the sand, eyes peeping above the surface. When a prey fish comes too near—it's up and snapping its jaws in a flash.

Sand devil

The flattened pectoral fins just below the head give this shark its name. They look like the wings of an angel if you use your imagination! Lying quietly on the seabed, this nocturnal ambush predator looks angelic until it lunges for a fish or to give a diver a nasty bite!

The angel shark's mouth is on the tip of the snout and contains some triangular, sharp teeth.

Angel sharks have whisker-like barbels to taste the water and to feel for the vibrations of prey.

NAME: *Squatina squatina* (skaty skate)
HABITAT: Seabed in coastal waters
DIET: Skates, rays, crustaceans, mollusks
LOCATION: Around Europe

Fallen angels

Sharks that lie still on the seabed are far too easy for human fishing trawlers to catch. That's why common angel sharks have almost been wiped out around Europe. Their last refuge is the Canary Islands off the coast of Africa.

BLUESPOTTED RIBBONTAIL

The ribbontail stingray looks like a big, blue-spotted pizza, with weird eyes on stalks. But you wouldn't want to be underneath it. It slides along the seabed and smothers its prey completely before eating it. And don't come too near it from behind, either. That spiny blue tail gives a warning—it's armed with a nasty venom.

Stingrays are mostly pretty docile, and won't harm you unless you go too near.

Make no bones

Stingrays can cover large areas of the seafloor like a blanket. They have no bones at all, just bendy cartilage, like the rubbery material in your nose. Unlike sharks and other fish, stingrays don't get their swimming power from their tail fin. They swim by rippling their big, flappy pectoral fins.

NAME: *Taeniura lymma*
(stripy tail ray)

HABITAT: Warm coastal waters and reefs

DIET: Shellfish, shrimp

LOCATION: Indian and Pacific

Little gel-filled pits, called "ampullae of Lorenzini," pick up the electrical fields of prey animals.

Rays and sharks

There are more than 200 different species of stingrays. Though they may not always look like it, rays are cousins of sharks because they both have skeletons made of rubbery cartilage. Sadly, 45 stingray species are now in danger of extinction, because of overfishing.

Panther ray

COOKIECUTTER SHARK

This small shark is named for a nasty way of wounding prey. It clamps its ring of razor-sharp teeth into a victim, twists around, and removes a plug of flesh like a cookie cutter removes cookie dough! Big fish, big sharks, and even whales can be wounded this way.

Fast food
By day, the cookiecutter lurks deep down. But at night, it comes up nearer the surface to hunt, hanging vertically, until some victim comes too close—then *whomp!* Bite, twist, and go!

The underside of the cookiecutter can glow, maybe to blend in with moonlight shining from above, fooling would-be victims.

Cookiecutters almost never attack humans, but they have attacked nuclear submarines!

NAME: *Isistius brasiliensis* (Brazilian equal sail)
HABITAT: Warm deep ocean waters
DIET: Lumps of flesh from big fish and whales
LOCATION: Worldwide

Teeth trash
The cookiecutter needs to keep the 25 to 31 teeth in its lower jaw super sharp. It regularly replaces them, losing the old set in one go and swallowing them to make the most of the nutrients.

VS KITEFIN SHARK

The kitefin shark glows! It's the world's biggest luminous animal with a backbone. But it mostly glows underneath, a blue-green that helps it vanish against the light-filled water above. It may be slow-moving, but its superpowerful bite makes it an efficient hunter in the deep waters where it lives.

The kitefin is a formidable predator, one of those weird little monsters of the deep like viperfish, dragonfish, lanternfish, scorpion fish, and many others.

Light liver!
The kitefin has a large liver filled with an oily liquid called "squalene." Squalene is less dense than water, so this helps the shark hover easily in mid water until prey comes by.

Like cookiecutters, kitefins can bite chunks out of much larger sharks and whales.

- **NAME:** *Dalatias licha* (greedy dalatiid)
- **HABITAT:** Areas of deep water
- **DIET:** Larger fish, sharks
- **LOCATION:** Worldwide

Family members
The kitefin shark is actually just one of ten small but furious sharks belonging to the kitefin family. They all have short, blunt snouts, and barrel-shaped bodies. The cookiecutter is also a kitefin.

Pygmy shark, kitefin family

LANTERN SHARK VS

Lantern sharks are the bright sparks of the shark world! The lantern shark's velvet belly is covered in glowing spots, which help it to vanish when seen from below by predators or prey. And glowing fin spines ward off predators that might strike from above, like lightsabers!

Lighting up
The natural glow of lantern sharks is called "bioluminescence" and is created by tiny organs called "photophores." These create a glow by a chemical reaction.

Some scientists believe the sharks use their glow to communicate with one another!

This shark has thin, smooth lips on a long, wide snout.

NAME: *Etmopterus spinax*
(bony wing spine)
HABITAT: Deep ocean margins
DIET: Small fish, crustaceans, squid
LOCATION: Eastern Atlantic, Mediterranean

Smallest shark
Probably the tiniest shark in the world is the dwarf lantern shark. It's smaller than many adults' hands, less than eight inches long! It's also capable of producing light from rows of photophores. Currently, it's known to live only in the Caribbean Sea.

SPINY DOGFISH

Spiny dogfish sharks may not be big, but they hunt in packs. Often, hundreds gang up to chase smaller fish such as herring, mackerel, and capelin, and even bigger sharks. They have sharp, venomous spines on their dorsal fins. If attacked, they arch their backs and inject venom into their attacker!

When hunting, a dogfish may ram prey with its pointy nose to stun it.

Spiny dogfish moms are pregnant for up to two years—longer than any other animal with a backbone.

Long-distance travelers
Spiny dogfish are record-breaking migrants. Scientists tagged one, and found it journeyed 5,000 miles, right across the Pacific from Washington State to Japan.

NAME: *Squalus acanthias* (spiny shark)
HABITAT: Warm coastal waters
DIET: Fish, squid, jellyfish
LOCATION: Worldwide except N. Pacific, polar, tropical

Fish and chips
Millions of pounds of spiny dogfish are caught every year. Especially in Europe, they're used as the fish in "fish and chips." The spiny dogfish was once the world's most common shark. But so many have been caught that it's in some danger of dying out.

SAWSHARK

BATTLE SCORE

Sawsharks are incredibly well armed, with slicing, sawlike snouts.

ATTACK SCORE: **7/10**
DEFENSE SCORE: **5/10**
LENGTH: **4.5 ft**
POWER MOVE: **Slashing**

Question: What's more terrifying than a shark with hundreds of sharp teeth? Answer: A shark with a long saw on its nose! Yes, the sawshark has a sawlike snout, or "rostrum," with 19 to 21 razor-sharp teeth on either side, used to slash prey and rip it to shreds.

Longnose sawsharks prefer sandy and gravelly beds between 130 and 2,000 feet down—too deep to bother swimmers.

Dangly barbels

The two moustache-like barbels dangling down either side of the saw are sensors. The sawshark trails them over the seabed to pick up signs of prey hiding in the sand. Once prey is detected, the sawshark digs it out of the sand with its saw, then slashes at it, to stun or kill it.

The sawteeth of a baby sawshark are folded when they are born to avoid hurting mom.

> **NAME:** *Pristiophorus cirratus* (saws with ringlets)
> **HABITAT:** Coastal seabeds
> **DIET:** Small fish, crustaceans
> **LOCATION:** Southern Australia

Sawshark or sawfish?

Sawsharks might look a little like small sawfish. But only the sawshark has barbels on its saw and five gill slits on the side of its head. And sawsharks never grow bigger than about 5 feet long.

VS SAWFISH

Sawfish are armed with a long, vicious saw on their snouts. On the biggest sawfish, the saw, or "rostrum," can be 6 to 8 feet long! Sawfish gash wounds into their prey, or pin victims against the seafloor. They look a little like sawsharks, but the sawfish is actually a ray, not a shark.

The teeth on the saw are all the same length and aren't replaced if they break off. The sawshark has long and short teeth on its saw, and replaces broken ones.

A sideways slash from the saw may cut a fish in half.

Sensitive saw
No one knows just how big sawfish grow. Big ones are likely to be more than 20 feet long, but there have been some reports of sawfish more than 30 feet long! The saw acts like an antenna. It is packed with ampullae of Lorenzini, which can pick up electrical signals emitted by prey under the seabed.

- **NAME:** *Pristis pectinata* (combed saw)
- **HABITAT:** Warm, coastal waters, estuaries
- **DIET:** Fish, shellfish
- **LOCATION:** Atlantic

Saw lovers
Sawfish have been symbols in many cultures for thousands of years. They have represented strength, war, protection, or connection to the ocean. But these incredible creatures have been badly overfished, and are now one of the ocean's most endangered creatures.

SAND TIGER SHARK

The sand tiger looks like a ferocious killer. It's quite large, with a mouthful of spiky teeth that you can see even when the mouth is closed! But actually, sand tigers rarely attack people, unless provoked. They swim around slowly in the water, waiting for smaller prey.

Sand tigers patrol close to the shore, frightening swimmers, but they rarely do any harm.

Gulp!
Sand tigers are the only sharks that come up for air. They don't breathe; they hold the air in their stomachs so they can float about looking for prey. They are named for hunting above the sands in the shallows—and for their tigerish appetite!

- **NAME:** *Carcharias taurus* (sharpened bull)
- **HABITAT:** Warm coastal waters, mainly reefs
- **DIET:** Fish, squid, crustaceans
- **LOCATION:** Worldwide, except Eastern Pacific

Net loss
In Australia and South Africa, nets were once put in the sea about 400 yards from shore to stop the sharks from coming in. But thousands of sand tigers were caught in the nets. And the sand tigers rarely harmed swimmers. So other ideas are now being tried to keep people safe.

VS SHORTFIN MAKO

The shortfin mako is the ocean's ultimate predator, built for high-speed action. Even superfast bluefin tuna and swordfish can't always get away from this Formula 1 racing shark. The shortfin mako can hit speeds of 45 mph or more in short bursts, and it sustains speeds of 25 mph for hour after hour, making it capable of running down almost any prey it chooses.

The mako's high performance is helped by keeping its body 45 degrees warmer than the water so its muscles work better.

High-jump champ
Makos are superathletes. They can not only swim very fast, but just like great whites, they can leap high into the air. No one knows why they breach, though they hunt by sight and might be spying out fish.

The mako is built for speed with a pointy snout, strong symmetrical tail, and stabilizing fins.

- **NAME:** *Isurus oxyrinchus* (balanced tail, pointy snout)
- **HABITAT:** Warm coastal, open ocean
- **DIET:** Fish, squid
- **LOCATION:** Worldwide

Marathon mako
The mako never stops moving. As well as being a champion sprinter, it's also a long-distance mover. It has two types of muscle: red muscle for long-distance swimming, and white muscle for sharp bursts of speed. That means even after a daylong swim, it may be ready for a short burst of action.

BLUE SHARK

BATTLE SCORE

Blue sharks are beautiful, big sharks and efficient hunters that are all too often caught in nets.

ATTACK SCORE: 6/10
DEFENSE SCORE: 6/10
LENGTH: Up to 13 ft
POWER MOVE:
Burst of speed

This metallic-blue shark with a white belly is perfectly camouflaged from above and below. It cruises around for thousands of miles, then puts on a big burst of speed when it spots a delicious squid, fish, smaller shark, or seabird in range. Sadly, as many as twenty million blue sharks are caught every year, and their fins sold for food.

Long, narrow pectoral fin.

Slim, torpedo-shaped body.

Orcas and shortfin mako prey on blue sharks.

- **NAME:** *Prionace glauca*
  (saw point, bluish)
- **HABITAT:** Cool waters of open ocean
- **DIET:** Mainly fish, squid
- **LOCATION:** Temperate, tropical oceans

Triangular teeth

Serrated teeth are good for cutting and for transferring bite force. The blue shark's upper teeth are curving triangles, with serrated edges. The teeth on the lower jaw are more finely serrated and symmetrical.

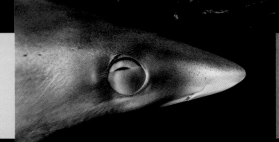

Extra eyelid

The blue shark, like many sharks, has a third eyelid called a "nictating membrane." It protects the eye when the shark is feeding and a prey animal may be struggling. Other sharks, like the great white, roll their eyes right back, exposing tough cartilage, for protection.

BULL SHARK

Alongside great whites and tiger sharks, bull sharks are known to attack humans. We're not a usual part of their diet, though. They're just more likely to come across us than other sharks, swimming in freshwater rivers and lakes as well as in the saltwater ocean. Fast and agile, bull sharks probably have the strongest bite force per square inch of any shark.

Bump-and-bite
Bull sharks generally hunt alone, in a specific territory. They often will headbutt their prey before an outright attack, sometimes bumping and biting their prey several times.

Pale to gray above, creamy below, these colors make for great camouflage.

- **NAME:** *Carcharhinus leucas* (sharp nose white)
- **HABITAT:** Shallow coastal waters, estuaries, rivers
- **DIET:** Fish, turtles, seabirds
- **LOCATION:** Tropical, subtropical oceans, rivers

Inland sharks
Bull sharks have been caught thousands of miles away from the ocean. One was found swimming 2,485 miles up the Amazon River. On their trips, they encounter other fierce predators. Crocs have been seen attacking bull sharks, and in Africa, bull sharks have been known to prey on young hippos.

GREENLAND SHARK

These massive sharks can grow to the size of a great white, but they are far less fierce. They live longer than any other animal with a backbone. Swimming slowly through the cold waters of the Arctic and North Atlantic, they eat other sharks, other fish, shellfish, and even reindeer and polar bears that have fallen through the ice and drowned.

Life in the cold
Greenland sharks have special chemicals, like antifreeze, to withstand near-freezing temperatures in cold, deep oceans. They are scavengers and will ambush prey. Rarely, they catch fast-swimming fish in a burst of speed.

Greenland sharks take about 100 years to become full adults!

These sharks may camp out near the breathing holes that seals carve in sea ice, and wait for dinner to come along!

NAME: *Somniosus microcephalus* (tiny head sleeper)
HABITAT: Deep, cold, coastal waters
DIET: Fish, sea mammals, birds, carrion
LOCATION: Northern Atlantic, Arctic

How old?!
In 2016, scientists examined the eyes of 28 Greenland sharks caught in fishing nets. Certain proteins in their eyes stay unchanged through life. So the scientists could radiocarbon-date them, and found one female shark could have been more than 400 years old!

VS GOBLIN SHARK

This strange and rare shark has a long, flat-topped head with a snout that's like a blade, and a long tail, like a thresher. You can see the nail-like teeth even when its mouth is closed. Its snout is covered with ampullae—electric sensors—and when it senses prey, it shoots out its jaws to snatch it!

Tengu
The name *goblin shark* is a translation of the Japanese name, *tenguzame*. *Tengu* are spirits with long noses, which can be good or bad, often shown with bright red faces.

Small fins probably make this shark a poor swimmer.

The shark is a pinkish color.

The jaws can extend almost to the end of the snout.

- **NAME:** *Mitsukurina owstoni* (named after Keigo Mitsukuri and Alan Owston)
- **HABITAT:** Deep water
- **DIET:** Fish, squid, crustaceans
- **LOCATION:** E. and W. Atlantic, Pacific, Indian

Ancient fish
Goblin sharks are often called "living fossils" because their species may date back 125 million years. The largest shark that ever lived is probably the Megalodon, which was alive between about 20 and 3.6 million years ago.

A swell shark does exactly what its name suggests! When threatened, it heads into a crevice and puffs itself up to double its regular size by swallowing water. It also bends its body into a U-shape, grabbing its tail fin in its mouth! Swell sharks belong to the catshark family of sleek, small sharks with catlike eyes and patterned skin.

The shark holds excess water in its stomach.

The sharks sometimes pile on top of each other when resting.

Shark that barks
After a threat is over, the swell shark relaxes its muscles, and expels the excess water with a sound that's like a dog bark!

Eyes are golden.

NAME: *Cephaloscyllium ventriosum* (swell-belly dogfish head)
HABITAT: Rocky coastal, kelp beds
DIET: Fish, crustaceans
LOCATION: Eastern Pacific

Way to glow
Swell sharks can change the ocean's blue light into a glowing green light in a process called "biofluorescence." No one really knows why these sharks glow, but it might help them see one another better, or attract a mate.

PORT JACKSON

It's easy to spot a Port Jackson shark because of the black markings that look like a harness. These sharks are also known as "oyster crushers" because of their unique teeth. The small front teeth have cusps to grip wriggling prey. The broad, flat, blunt back teeth are used for crushing and grinding shells. Unusually, Port Jackson sharks can eat and breathe at the same time!

Each dorsal fin has a spine in front of it.

Splurge!
The Port Jackson shark regurgitates unwanted food, or pushes its stomach out through its mouth to expel it!

NAME: *Heterodontus portusjacksoni* (other teeth Port Jackson)
HABITAT: Temperate coastal, intertidal
DIET: Mostly echinoderms such as sea urchins, sea stars, crustaceans
LOCATION: Coast of W. and S. Australia, Tasmania

The blunt head has a small mouth.

Amazing eggs
The female Port Jackson shark lays eggs shaped like spirals, about 6 inches long. She carries the eggs in her mouth, and wedges them into a crevice in the rock, where they harden. A shark pup emerges from each egg 10 to 12 months later.

OCEANIC WHITETIP SHARK

Living far out to sea, the oceanic whitetip is rarely spotted and is very mysterious. Though it doesn't come to shore, when a ship sinks, survivors may be in trouble. It's big and strong, and may hunt in packs.

Neck-and-neck
When whitetips charge in one after another on prey, it looks like a mad feeding frenzy. But really, the sharks are working together, taking turns to strike, and sharing food. The famous diver Jacques Cousteau insisted whitetips are "the most dangerous of all sharks."

The shark gets its name from the white tips on its fins.

Oceanic whitetips are in danger of extinction, killed by humans in huge numbers for their fins.

NAME: *Carcharhinus longimanus* (sharp nose, long hand)
HABITAT: Warm, surface waters of open ocean
DIET: Big fish, squid, seabirds
LOCATION: Worldwide

Shark tragedy
When the battleship USS *Indianapolis* was sunk by torpedo in 1945, 890 crewmembers managed to get off before it went down. Only 316 survived to be picked up later. Some believe hundreds were killed by oceanic whitetip sharks in the worst shark attack ever.

VS MANTIS SHRIMP

These technicolor shrimp are possibly no bigger than your hand. But they have a genuine superpower—a punch with the force of a bullet. With their club-like arms, they can smash right through an aquarium wall or knock a crab's claws off.

A hermit crab might hide in its shell, but the mantis shrimp can smash the shell to bits.

Male mantis shrimp sometimes fight and punch holes in one another.

Watch out!
When threatened, a mantis shrimp rears up, arms bristling, with large spots looking like giant eyes. This is called a "meral spread." The shrimp punches at over 50 mph and with 10,000 times the force of gravity, and the water around it heats up to the temperature of the surface of the sun!

NAME: *Odontodactylus scyllarus* (toothfinger crab)
HABITAT: Sand near coral reefs
DIET: Crustaceans, mollusks
LOCATION: Western Pacific, Indian

Superb sight
Superman, eat your heart out! Mantis shrimp have eyes even more amazing than their punch. It's possible that they can interpret colors without input from the brain, as they have more color receptors than we do, positioned in a special way on their retinas.

BLIND SHARK

This little shark of the shallows is so hardy that it can survive in a fish tank. It isn't really blind, but shuts its eyes when taken out of water. Amazingly, it can survive out of water for 18 hours, useful if it gets stranded by the tide going out! It hunts on the seabed, in water barely deep enough to cover it.

Night and day

This nocturnal hunter hides in caves or crevices during the day, though it's even been spotted resting on sponges! When disturbed, it stays still or may bury itself more deeply.

The shark is brown with small white spots.

* **NAME:** *Brachaelurus waddi* (short cat war club)
* **HABITAT:** Shallow seas on rocky coasts
* **DIET:** Small fish, crustaceans, squid
* **LOCATION:** Eastern Australia

Carpet sharks, like the blind shark, move sluggishly over the seafloor.

A bit like catfish

The scientific name for blind sharks, *Brachaelurus*, means "short cat." That's because the pair of long, sensory barbels on their snouts make them look like catfish. The barbels help to detect prey.

Catfish

VS VENUS COMB

This little predator of the shallows threatens sharks or rays many times its size. It doesn't move fast—it's a snail—but with rows of spines like big combs, it doesn't have to. To get to the soft parts of its prey, it drills a hole through the shell and uses its teeth to scrape out the flesh.

The snail may bury itself in sand, with its taillike siphon above the surface, taking in water for breathing and sensing prey.

Combing the seabed
There are more than a hundred spines in the combs. They don't only provide protection; they also stop the snail from sinking into soft sand.

NAME: *Murex pecten* (mussel comb)
HABITAT: Warm, shallow waters
DIET: Shellfish
LOCATION: Indian, Western Pacific

Imperial snail
One relative of the venus comb was famous in ancient Rome. Drops of slime from its glands made a rich purple dye. It took a hundred thousand snails to dye a small piece of cloth, and the color was used to dye the robes of the emperors.

MANTA RAY

 VS

With two big "horns" and a dark, cape-like shape, the giant manta ray is sometimes called the "devil fish." But it's completely harmless, flapping its triangular, big pectoral fins to swim steadily at up to 22 mph, using the lobes on either side of its mouth to funnel in water filled with plankton.

Speedy escape
Giant manta rays are great swimmers with few natural predators. Sharks may take a bite, but only a few superpredators, such as orcas, can catch them. Sadly, human fishing has put them in danger of extinction.

Mantas feed in wonderful ways, including doing barrel rolls like somersaults and going piggyback!

The long, whiplike tail lacks the venomous spines seen in stingrays.

NAME: *Mobula birostris* (giant manta)
HABITAT: Open ocean, coastal
DIET: Zooplankton
LOCATION: Warm waters worldwide

Ray brain
Giant manta rays may be the smartest of all fish. They've got a brain ten times bigger than a whale shark's and are playful and curious. Like only a few other animals, such as great apes and dolphins, manta rays may even recognize themselves in a mirror.

BARRACUDA

Ferocious barracuda fish are long and streamlined, with powerful tails, rapid acceleration, and sharp, pointed teeth. They rarely attack humans, though they hunt using sight, and may mistake the glint of a diver's belt for a delicious little anchovy!

Barracuda battery
Young barracuda swim in large groups called a "battery," but older fish break away and hunt alone. Females usually grow larger than males. When they've eaten enough, barracuda may herd prey into the shallows and guard them for an easy snack later.

Barracuda bite prey in half or swallow small prey whole.

- **NAME:** *Sphyraena* (like a pike)
- **HABITAT:** Shallows, including mangroves and reefs
- **DIET:** Mainly fish, squid, shrimp
- **LOCATION:** Warm waters worldwide

Like a pike
The barracuda's large head and long, fang-filled jaws look rather like the notorious river predator the pike. Its scientific name *Sphyraena* actually means "like a pike."

Pike

BOX JELLYFISH VS

The Australian box jellyfish has 10-foot-long tentacles covered with thousands of tiny, explosive cells. When alerted by chemicals in its victim's skin, these fire out darts of venom that cause agonizing pain, and can kill a human in under five minutes. One box jellyfish has enough venom to kill sixty adults.

Pale blue and transparent, box jellyfish are hard to spot.

They are named for the cube shape of their bell.

Jellyfish have no brain; they rely on nerves to coordinate behavior.

- **NAME:** *Chironex fleckeri* (Flecker's handkiller)
- **HABITAT:** Warm, tropical, coastal waters
- **DIET:** Fish, crustaceans, worms
- **LOCATION:** Papua New Guinea, Vietnam, Philippines, Australia

I see you
Unlike other jellyfish, box jellyfish can swim, rather than just drift. They have clusters of six eyes at four corners. No one knows exactly how they see. But some experts think that they watch and actively chase prey.

Lucky escape
In 2010, ten-year-old Rachael Shardlow found her legs wrapped with box jellyfish tentacles when swimming in the sea in Queensland, Australia. Her brother pulled her out of the water half-conscious, and people nearby applied vinegar, which made the tentacles withdraw. Amazingly, she survived!

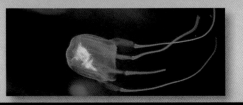

LION'S MANE JELLYFISH

The mouth is situated on the bell's underside.

The world's biggest jellyfish is named for its huge fringe of brown tentacles. Its bell is the size of a car, and weighs up to a ton. It has 1,200 or so tentacles, in eight clusters, each possibly as long as a blue whale! It stretches out its tentacles to trap fish, crustaceans, or other jellyfish, then stuns them with its venom.

Solo traveler

The lion's mane prefers cold water, but individuals can drift long distances and end up in all kinds of places. Most of these jellies swim alone, but in stormy seas, they may gather in a swarm. Big swarms can shut down beaches for hundreds of miles.

The jelly produces light and can glow underwater.

- **NAME:** *Cyanea capillata* (blue hair)
- **HABITAT:** Surface waters
- **DIET:** Fish, crustaceans, small jellyfish
- **LOCATION:** Cold northern waters

Doing well

The impact of human activity on the oceans—overfishing, pollution, and warming temperatures—has been terrible for its animals. But this jellyfish has managed to thrive because so many of its predators and competitors have disappeared.

Leopard seals are named for their spotted coats. Just like leopards on land, they are strong, fast, sleek predators with big jaws. They eat krill, fish, and squid. But they also prey on smaller seals and wait on the edges of icy shores to pounce on unlucky penguins as they plunge into the water. Only orcas will attack adult leopard seals.

Smashed penguins
Leopard seals fling penguins to and fro and smash them against the water's surface. Eventually the penguin bursts open and the seal digs in!

Males sing while underwater, maybe to attract a mate or warn other males from their territory!

- **NAME:** *Hydrurga leptonyx* (small-clawed water worker)
- **HABITAT:** Rocky and icy coasts
- **DIET:** Fish, squid, seals, penguin, krill
- **LOCATION:** Antarctica

Leopard seals are mostly loners.

My seal teacher
In 2006, photographer Paul Nicklen sat on the Antarctic ice to photograph seals. But one female leopard seal thought he was starving, so she brought him dead and wounded penguins, possibly to try to teach him how to hunt!

ELEPHANT SEAL

Elephant seals are the world's largest meat-eating mammals, except for whales. A big male elephant seal can weigh over 3 tons! No wonder they move so slowly. On land, they lumber along at less-than-human walking pace, and even in the water, they can barely reach 3 mph.

- **NAME:** *Mirounga leonina* (lionlike seal)
- **HABITAT:** Deep coastal waters
- **DIET:** Mainly squid, fish
- **LOCATION:** Southern Ocean, Antarctic peninsula, subantarctic islands

Killer targets

These seals are too big for most hunters to take on, though great whites and orcas are fierce and fast enough to prey on them. Skilled divers, they hoover prey off the seafloor.

An elephant seal can dive more than a mile deep and hold its breath for more than an hour.

Useful trunk

Elephant seals are named for the male's elephant-trunk-like snout. This helps the seal make a huge roar. It is also a water-capture device. When it's on dry land for long periods during the mating season, an elephant seal's snout is used to reabsorb the moisture when it breathes out.

GIANT MORAY EEL

Giant moray eels look like monster snakes with huge heads and vicious teeth. But these smooth, slinky predators are fish, with small fins. They have a second set of jaws, which shoot forward and grasp prey, then retract, pulling the prey into their mouth. For fish living around coral reefs, giant morays are enemy number one!

Morays may be attacked by barracudas and sharks.

When a moray eel's jaws gape wide, it's just breathing, not preparing to bite!

Night hunters
Morays hide in coral reefs during the day and venture out at night to hunt, detecting prey through the chemicals they give off, rather than by sight.

A coating of oily slime protects the skin as the eel slithers through the coral.

- **NAME:** *Gymnothorax javanicus* (bare-chested Javanese)
- **HABITAT:** Lagoons, coral reefs
- **DIET:** Fish, crustaceans
- **LOCATION:** Indian, Pacific

Hunting buddies
The giant moray and the roving coral grouper sometimes hunt together. The grouper signals to the eel as if to say, "Go!" The grouper points out where something tasty is hiding in the reef, and the moray moves in, flushing out other prey for the grouper.

VS SWORDFISH

Swordfish are one of the ocean's fastest predator fish. They shoot through the water at up to 60 mph, sometimes breaching into the air. Their long, flat, swordlike bills slash side to side to wound or stun larger prey. Smaller prey get swallowed whole! Like moray eels, they have few natural predators, though orcas and shortfin makos will sometimes take them on.

Big growth
Swordfish start as tiny fry but grow fast, putting on a million times their own weight during their lives. Their sword starts to grow soon after hatching.

Swordfish belong to a group of fish called "billfish." They're the only billfish to have flat and blunt rather than round and pointed bills.

Special cells in the eye and a fatty layer keep the eyes and brain warm in cold water.

- **NAME:** *Xiphias gladius* (swordy sword)
- **HABITAT:** Warm surface waters, sometimes cooler
- **DIET:** Large fish such as bluefish, squid
- **LOCATION:** Indian, Pacific, Atlantic

Ocean travelers
Swordfish migrate thousands of miles every year, to warmer waters in winter and cooler waters in summer. Their bodies are suited to short bursts of speed. For long journeys, they're helped by currents.

STONEFISH

The stonefish is the ultimate camouflage ninja, looking just like a weed-covered stone. It is also the world's most venomous fish. The spines on its back can inject deadly venom like a hypodermic needle into the foot of any human swimmer unlucky enough to tread on one, causing agonizing pain and maybe death in under an hour.

The 13 spines on the stonefish's back are all venomous.

NAME: *Synanceia verrucosa* (with veins and warty)
HABITAT: Warm shallow waters around reefs
DIET: Small fish, shrimp
LOCATION: Red Sea, Indian, Pacific

So long, sucker
The stonefish lies perfectly disguised on the seabed until a prey fish comes too close. Then *whoosh!* Like a high-powered vacuum cleaner, it sucks in its victim in a hundredth of a second.

Antivenom
If you suffer a stonefish sting, a quick dose of antivenom may save your life. But to make it, brave divers must "milk" venom from live stonefish. The milked venom is injected in safe quantities into a horse, and the horse's body reacts to make the antivenom.

LIONFISH

Lionfish get their name from the intimidating array of spiny fins, or "rays," like a lion's mane. These rays scare off all but the bravest predators—and eighteen of them contain a powerful venom. A sting can be very painful, and rarely, fatal. Lionfish also have a huge mouth for engulfing small prey.

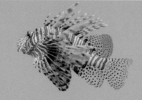

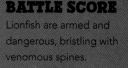

Striped out
The lionfish's bold stripes break up the fish's outline, so it's hard to tell what is fish and what is venomous spine.

Lionfish may shoot out jets of water that confuse or stun prey fish, making them easy to catch.

The stomach can expand up to 30 times its size to take in food to feed the lionfish for days.

NAME: *Pterois miles* (winged soldier)
HABITAT: Warm coastal waters
DIET: Small fish, crustaceans
LOCATION: Indian Ocean and Red Sea

Lion invasion
Some Americans who tried to keep lionfish as pets let them go into the Atlantic. With no natural predators, lionfish multiplied rapidly all the way down the east coast of the Americas, from Delaware to Brazil. This killed off many of the local fish.

ANGLERFISH

Fish don't get much more extreme than humpback anglerfish, sometimes called "black sea devils." Their power comes from a light, made by glowing bacteria, that they dangle on a modified ray above their heads like a fishing rod, luring prey into their mouths or attracting a mate.

Female lure
Only female anglerfish have glowing lures. Some males move from female to female. Some mate for life and never eat, so they don't need a lure!

A gigantic mouth and daggerlike teeth make sure it traps any prey that floats by.

- **NAME:** *Melanocetus johnsonii* (Johnson's black sea devil)
- **HABITAT:** Deep water
- **DIET:** Fish
- **LOCATION:** Tropical, temperate oceans

Monkfish

Living at depth
The humpback is just one of more than 200 kinds of anglerfish. They mostly live in deep water, but the humpback lives in the deepest waters of them all. There's a fish called the "angler" or "monkfish," which also uses a lure, but is much bigger than an anglerfish and lives in shallow water.

VS GIANT GROUPER

BATTLE SCORE
One of the biggest bony fish on the reef, the biggest threat to groupers is humans.

ATTACK SCORE: **6/10**
DEFENSE SCORE: **7/10**
LENGTH: **6–9 ft**
POWER MOVE:
Big mouth

Giant groupers are so big, they can weigh 880 pounds, the same as five adult humans! They live in underwater caves, in shipwrecks, or under ledges in coral reefs, waiting to ambush prey. They cram all kinds of things into their giant mouths, including baby turtles and small sharks.

Groupers live for a long time, up to 50 years.

Solitary hunter
Groupers spend most of their lives alone, lurking in dark places, waiting to ambush prey. Some have a preference for spiny lobsters and crabs. The grouper's muscular jaws easily crush the shells of their prey.

You can tell the age of a grouper from the annual growth rings in its dorsal fin rays, similar to tree rings.

- **NAME:** *Epinephelus lanceolatus* (cloudy and armed with a lance)
- **HABITAT:** Warm coastal waters, reefs, estuaries
- **DIET:** Varied: mostly fish, crustaceans
- **LOCATION:** Indian, Pacific

Grouper family
How young groupers live is still a big secret, as they are rarely seen while growing up in the reef. What is known is that some groupers change from female to male as they grow older.

FLAMBOYANT CUTTLEFISH

 VS

Pfeffer's flamboyant cuttlefish lives up to its name. It's tiny but looks incredible! When threatened, this little creature doesn't run away like other cuttlefish. It flashes through colors like a Times Square light display. Any predator should heed the warning: it's one of the most poisonous animals in the ocean.

The cuttlefish is dark brown, white, and yellow, with purple-pink arms. When alarmed, it flashes maroon, black, blue, and red!

Cuttlebone
Cuttlefish are mollusks, like clams, but they have no shells. They have a cuttlebone to help them to float. This cuttlefish only has a small cuttlebone, which is probably why it mostly walks, using 8 arms!

- **NAME:** *Metasepia pfefferi* (Pfeffer's extra cuttlefish)
- **HABITAT:** Shallow water over mud and sand flats
- **DIET:** Fish, crustaceans
- **LOCATION:** Northern Australia, Papua New Guinea, Indonesia

Shots of ink
When attacked, most cuttlefish can squirt out a cloud of dark ink to confuse the predator and make an escape. The ink from cuttlefish was used long ago for writing. The brown color, "sepia," comes from the Latin name for a cuttlefish.

BLUE-RINGED OCTOPUS

A cousin of the cuttlefish in the cephalopod family, the greater blue-ringed octopus is also beautiful, intelligent, and totally deadly! It's mostly calm, but if alarmed, it bites attackers and injects a deadly venom into the wound.

The octopus pierces its prey's shell with its horny beak, injects venom, then picks out the meat.

Beware the blue light

When alarmed, the octopus turns yellow and flashes its blue rings on and off, as a warning. Despite its tiny size, it has enough venom in its salivary glands to kill 26 fully grown humans in minutes.

- **NAME:** *Hapalochlaena lunulata* (delicately ringed cloak)
- **HABITAT:** Coral, rocky, sandy pools
- **DIET:** Crabs and shrimp
- **LOCATION:** Eastern Indian, Western Pacific

Deadly poison

The octopus's bite is painless, and divers may not know when they are bitten. But there is no known antidote, and they may die in only fifteen minutes. People bitten in a tidal pool close to shore can be given emergency treatment, and may survive if they are very lucky.

DEEP-SEA LIZARDFISH VS

Multiple rows of needlelike teeth and a wide crocodile gape make the deep-sea lizardfish a true terror of the deep. It lives more than 3,000 feet below in the cold darkness, lying in wait. Food is scarce at these depths, so it will even eat the bodies of dead animals that float down from above.

Lizardfish can get so desperate for food, they eat one another.

Gotcha!
The lizardfish gets its name because it looks just like a lizard. Most of the time, it lies motionless on the seafloor, sometimes partly buried, its jaw slightly raised. But if prey comes too close, it can make a lightning-fast lunge—and snap!

The deep-sea lizardfish has big, green eyes that help it to see its prey.

NAME: *Bathysaurus ferox*
(fierce deep-sea lizard)
HABITAT: Deep water
DIET: Fish, crustaceans, animal corpses
LOCATION: Atlantic, Indian, Southern Pacific

Energy store
The deep-sea lizardfish has a liver that is about 20 percent of its body weight. Scientists aren't completely sure why, but it seems likely that it's an energy store, used when food is hard to find.

GIANT SQUID

The giant squid is the ultimate monster of the deep. A huge, 30-foot tentacle shoots out to snatch prey, and hauls it toward the mouth and its sharp, central beak. There it rips its victims to shreds with its tongue-like "radula," coated with rows of teeth.

The giant squid has the largest eyes of any animal— at over 1 foot wide.

No escape
The squid not only has two very long tentacles but eight shorter arms for grasping prey. They are all lined on the inside with powerful suckers ringed with sawlike blades.

The brain is shaped like a donut, with a hole in the middle through which its esophagus passes!

- **NAME:** *Architeuthis dux* (top squid chief)
- **HABITAT:** Deep water
- **DIET:** Fish, shrimp, other squid
- **LOCATION:** Worldwide

You've got to be squidding!
Giant squids live so deep that they are rarely seen, though legends of giant sea monsters have been around since ancient times. It was only in 2006 that a giant squid was caught, so scientists could see it and examine it for real.

SAILFISH

You can't mistake a sailfish. It has a long, pointed bill and a big sail-like fin on its back. It's also one of the fastest fish of the ocean, with some experts saying that it can reach speeds in excess of 68 mph. It belongs to a family of fish with spear-like bills, including other superspeedy fish, like the marlin.

Its color changes from blue to silver to almost black, with orange and blue spots and bars when it's about to attack.

The pointed bill is actually the sailfish's upper jaw.

- **NAME:** *Istiophorus platypterus* (sail-bearing broad wing)
- **HABITAT:** Open ocean, subtropical and tropical
- **DIET:** Mainly fish and squid
- **LOCATION:** Worldwide

Round up
Sailfish hunt in packs, working together like wolves to drive shoals of fish up through the water. They raise their sail fins both to aid quick turns and to herd the prey into a tighter ball. When the ball is tight enough, some sailfish stay herding, but others are the strikers, darting in one by one to slash this way and that to injure fish, preparing them to be eaten.

Caught for sport
It is illegal to catch these amazing fish commercially for food, but they are still caught for sport. The sailfish puts up a powerful struggle when it's hooked, which makes them a challenge to land.

VS BLUEFIN TUNA

The Atlantic bluefin tuna is as big as a polar bear and swallows its prey whole. It's hundreds of pounds of muscle—a big bluefin can weigh 1,500 pounds. It's also one of the strongest, fastest fish in the ocean, almost as fast as billfish like the sailfish and marlin.

Great adaptations
The tuna's warm blood means that it can cope very well in cold seas as well as warm. This fish's body has a way of holding on to body heat generated by its muscles. That warmth helps it to see better, swim faster, and act smarter so it can thrive in deep, cool waters.

The fins fold into a groove when the fish is swimming fast, to keep it streamlined.

- **NAME:** *Thunnus thynnus* (tunny tuna)
- **HABITAT:** Open ocean
- **DIET:** Fish, squid, crustaceans
- **LOCATION:** Atlantic, Mediterranean

Despite its large size, the bluefin eats mostly small fish, because it gulps them in whole, on the move.

Million-dollar fish
The tuna's large size and tasty flesh have made it a target for fishing. In 2019, a single 600-pound, 8-foot bluefin tuna sold for 3 million dollars. Numbers are growing since limits were put on its fishing.

PORTUGUESE VS MAN O' WAR

The Portuguese man o' war is a floating stinging machine with venomous tendrils. The tendrils won't kill humans but they can sting—and they sting even when dead. The man o' war looks like a jellyfish, but is in fact a siphonophore—made of a group of animals called "zooids."

- **NAME:** *Physalia physalis* (windy bladder)
- **HABITAT:** Tropical, subtropical waters
- **DIET:** Fish, invertebrates
- **LOCATION:** Open ocean worldwide

Strong winds can blow swarms of these animals ashore. Stay away.

Drifting by
The tendrils hang from a transparent, bag-like float filled with gas. The bag just drifts with the current or the wind, but can deflate to submerge briefly to escape threats on the surface.

Named for looking a little like an 18th-century Portuguese warship in sail!

Got your sting
The blue ocean slug has no fear of the Portuguese man o' war's stinging tendrils. It attacks and eats them, including the stinging cells. Then it sends the stinging cells it has swallowed to the tips of its tendrils to create its own stinging weapons.

BLUE WHALE

The blue whale is the biggest creature of all time. Its tongue weighs around 3 tons, and its heart weighs 1,000 pounds. Its brain is six times bigger than ours, and it's smart! It's hard to tell how smart, but blue whales are skilled navigators, expert at targeting shallow, dense krill swarms to maximize the amount of food it gets using the least energy.

Boom Boom!
Blue whales are really, really loud—louder than a jet plane—and can be heard hundreds of miles away. Both sexes make single-note sounds. Males are noisier, and sing as they make very deep dives.

In summer, blue whales head for cold polar waters to fill up on krill. Then they migrate thousands of miles to warm tropical waters to mate and give birth to the biggest of all animal babies!

Filter feeder
Despite their vast size, blue whales only eat tiny shrimplike krill—40 million a day! They gulp in an amount of water heavier than they are, and sieve out the krill through the hundreds of baleen plates in their mouths.

- **NAME:** *Balaenoptera musculus* (winged whale muscular)
- **HABITAT:** Temperate and colder waters
- **DIET:** Krill
- **LOCATION:** All oceans except Arctic

Hunted by humans
About 100 years ago, blue whales were hunted by humans. Their hunting was banned in 1966. Only about 15,000 blue whales are alive today, 90 percent fewer than 100 years ago.

Glossary

baleen plates in the mouth of a whale that filter and trap food

barbel fleshy, whisker-like organ near the mouth of a fish

bioluminescence light produced from a living thing

breach to break through the surface of water

carrion flesh of dead animals

camouflage hide or disguise by blending into surroundings

cartilage strong, smooth material in animal bodies that is more flexible than bone

caudal fin tail fin, located at the end of a fish

cephalopod group of animals that includes octopus and squid

crustacean group of animals that includes crabs, lobsters, and shrimp

dermal denticles toothlike scales that cover a shark

dorsal fin fin on the back of a fish or whale

extinct died out, no longer existing

flukes the parts of the tail of dolphins and whales

fry a young fish

gill part of the body that helps fish "breathe" underwater; humans get oxygen to live by breathing air, whereas fish get the oxygen they need from water

kelp type of seaweed

krill tiny shrimplike creature

lateral line line along the side of a fish consisting of organs that sense pressure and vibration

lagoon shallow body of water separated from a larger body of water

luminous giving off light in the dark

mangrove shrub or tree that grows in swamps

migrate move from one region or habitat to another

mollusk animal with a soft body that lives in wet habitats, including snails and octopus

pectoral fin fin located on either side of a fish near the gills

photophores organ in fish that produces light

placenta organ in a pregnant animal that provides nutrients to the growing baby

plankton tiny organisms that drift in water

pod group of dolphins or whales

radiocarbon dating a scientific method for determining the age of something

regurgitate bring up swallowed food back into the mouth

rostrum a beak or beaklike part, such as the saws of sawsharks and sawfish

scavenger animal that feeds on carrion

serrated having a jagged edge like a saw

siphon tubelike organ that draws in and expels water

tentacle thin, flexible limb used to move, grasp, and sense

temperate having mild temperatures

Index

Credits

Photos ©: cover bottom left: Brett Phibbs/Image Source on Offset/Shutterstock; back cover top left: Wildestanimal/Alamy Stock Photo; back cover bottom left: Frhojdysz/Dreamstime; back cover bottom right: WaterFrame/Alamy Stock Photo; 2-3: Martin Voeller/Dreamstime; 4-5: hansgertbroeder/Getty Images; 4 bottom right: Nature Picture Library/Alamy Stock Photo; 6-7 bottom: richcarey/Getty Images; 7 bottom left: Jeff Rotman/Alamy Stock Photo; 7 bottom center: HKPNC/Getty Images; 7 vision: BrendanHunter/Getty Images; 7 smell: Violetastock/Getty Images; 7 taste: RainervonBrandis/Getty Images; 7 hearing: Nicola Geneletti/Getty Images; 8 top fin: Sitade/Getty Images; 8 background: IBorisoff/Getty Images; 8 background: dwphotos/Getty Images; 8 background: FlashMovie/Getty Images; 8 background: richcarey/Getty Images; 8 whale shark: Andrea Izzotti/Getty Images; 8 tuna: Nature Picture Library/Alamy Stock Photo; 8 giant squid: by wildestanimal/Getty Images; 8 lizard fish: Pally/Alamy Stock Photo; 8 goblin shark: Kelvin Aitken/VWPics/Alamy Stock Photo; 8 dumbo octopus: NOAA/Alamy Stock Photo; 8 anglerfish: Marko Steffensen/Alamy Stock Photo; 10 center: Pieter De Pauw/Getty Images; 10 bottom: Howard Chen/Getty Images; 12-13 background: richcarey/Getty Images; 14 center: Frhojdysz/Dreamstime; 14 bottom: Janos Rautonen/Alamy Stock Photo; 17 center: BIOSPHOTO/Alamy Stock Photo; 18-19 center: valio84sl/Getty Images; 18 bottom left: indianoceanimagery/Getty Images; 20 background: yannp/Getty Images; 21 bottom: Blue Planet Archive/Alamy Stock Photo; 23 center: Jeff Rotman/Alamy Stock Photo; 24 center: Pally/Alamy Stock Photo; 24 bottom right: Doug Perrine/Alamy Stock Photo; 25 center: Pally/Alamy Stock Photo; 25 bottom right: Nature Picture Library/Alamy Stock Photo; 26 center: Andy Murch/BluePlanetArchive; 26 bottom right: USNM 206093, Division of Fishes, Smithsonian Institution, Photo by Chip Clark; 27 background: Dirk Jan Mattaar/Dreamstime; 28 center: Stephen Frink Collection/Alamy Stock Photo; 28 bottom right: Stephen Frink Collection/Alamy Stock Photo; 29 center: solarworksart/Getty Images; 29 bottom right: tbradford/Getty Images; 32 bottom left: Nature Picture Library/Alamy Stock Photo; 33 center: June Jacobsen/Getty Images; 34 bottom right: louise murray/Alamy Stock Photo; 35 bottom right: John Hughes for Scholastic Inc.; 35 center: Kelvin Aitken/VWPics/Alamy Stock Photo; 36 center: Mark Conlin/Alamy Stock Photo; 36 bottom right: Dorling Kindersley ltd/Alamy Stock Photo; 38 center: NaluPhoto/Getty Images; 40 center: Jeff Rotman/Alamy Stock Photo; 41 bottom right: World History Archive/Alamy Stock Photo; 48 bottom left: Reinhard Dirscherl/ullstein bild/Getty Images; 48 bottom right: imageBROKER/Alamy Stock Photo; 49 center: Pally/Alamy Stock Photo; 52 center: Marko Steffensen/Alamy Stock Photo; 56 center: Pally/Alamy Stock Photo; 56 bottom right: David Shale/Naturepl.com; 57 center: Akinobu Kimura; 58 center: Nature Picture Library/Alamy Stock Photo; 59 center: Nature Picture Library/Alamy Stock Photo; 61 center: Nature Picture Library/Alamy Stock Photo; 61 bottom: Nature Picture Library/Alamy Stock Photo; 62-63: HakBak1979/Getty Images. All other photos © Shutterstock.com.

Copyright

ISBN 978-1-338-82877-1

10 9 8 7 6 5 4 3 2 1   22 23 24 25 26

Printed in China   173

First edition 2022

Cover design by Neal Cobourne: our-kid-design.com
Book design by Victoria Gordon-Harris